IMAGES
of America

HANOVER
NEW HAMPSHIRE

Looking at the village and college from Norwich, Vermont, in 1906.

IMAGES
of America

HANOVER
NEW HAMPSHIRE

Frank J. Barrett Jr.

ARCADIA

First published 1997
Copyright © Frank J. Barrett Jr., 1997

ISBN 0-7524-0571-3

Published by Arcadia Publishing,
an imprint of the Chalford Publishing Corporation,
One Washington Center, Dover, New Hampshire 03820.
Printed in Great Britain

Library of Congress Cataloging-in-Publication Data applied for

Contents

Acknowledgments

All of the images contained within the pages of this book are from the author's private collection, accumulated from many sources over many years, except those photographs on pages 32B, 42T, 102T, and 103B that appear courtesy of Dartmouth College Archives Special Collections.

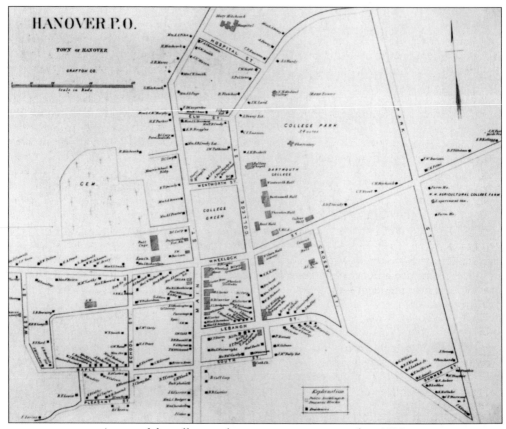

A map of the village and campus area as it existed in 1892.

Introduction

This book does not pretend to be an illustrated history of the town of Hanover and Dartmouth College, nor an architectural treatise of the same. Rather, these pages present a brief glimpse of a very special place in history between the years 1900 and 1950—when the modern village and college, still visible today, first evolved into view.

Almost all of the images contained herein are postcard views that portray this unique community as it chose to exhibit itself to the world. And, combined with these images, the author has attempted to provide the reader with as much authenticated history as limited space allows.

The last seven years of the nineteenth century were part of a watershed decade for the village of Hanover and Dartmouth College. The 1880s saw several devastating fires ravage the village area—respectively laying waste to property along both Lebanon Street and South Main Street. And the college, a small regional school of about three hundred students, experienced a painful period of academic upheaval and unrest. But in 1893, the village and the college jointly constructed a modern water supply system so that the devastation of earlier years would hopefully never be felt on the same scale again. That same year, Dartmouth College installed William Jewett Tucker, Class of 1861, as the ninth president of the 124-year-old institution.

The new reservoir was the first of many modern village improvements that would usher Hanover into the twentieth century, and it was President Tucker who, realizing that the school had to grow in order to survive, began the evolutionary process of taking Dartmouth College from a small regional New England school to the world-renowned college that it is today. In a seemingly brief amount of time, the dusty backwater village that unabashedly still shows its colonial roots gave way to a community of shade-tree-lined streets and buildings of fresh architectural flourish. Brick multi-storied business blocks replaced older wood-framed dwellings on Main Street, and new academic buildings of substantial bearing forever recast the picturesque pre-Revolutionary appearance of the green. Hence, the new century dawned on the Hanover Plain with a frenzy of building activity and optimism that well matched the ideals of the nation's new president—the young and energetic Theodore Roosevelt. These were to be good years.

President Tucker had the foresight to establish a master plan, the first ever for the college, and during the sixteen years of his administration (1893–1909), additional land was aggressively acquired by Dartmouth. Fourteen new buildings were erected around the campus in addition to six already existing structures that were extensively renovated to better suit the needs of the rapidly expanding institution. Charles A. Rich, Dartmouth Class of 1875 and a principal in the well-known architectural firm of Lamb & Rich located in New York City, was selected as the college's architect. Rich's relationship with his alma mater would endure for about twenty years and serve to grace the campus with nineteen impressive structures designed in the then-fashionable Neoclassical style.

With the new growth of the college, so too did the village begin to spread outward—first along the newly subdivided area of Webster Avenue and Occom Ridge, and then to the west of the School Street area as well as along both North and South Park Streets. By the 1920s, the farm fields south of the village and Lebanon Street would begin to sprout buildings as further growth took place. South Main Street continued to fill out, losing more of the reminders of its earlier past, while modern municipal improvements continued to make life easier and cleaner for the village's inhabitants. And, by the early 1920s, the village began more and more to accommodate the automobile, as new methods of mass production in far-off industrial centers vastly increased its popularity and general availability.

Ernest Fox Nichols, an accomplished and internationally noted physics professor from Columbia University, followed Mr. Tucker as college president and continued forward with the work started by his predecessor's administration. During Mr. Nichols' term in office (1909–1916), six major new buildings were added to the campus under his direction, and 45 acres of land extending from North Main Street down to the Connecticut River were acquired from the Hitchcock family. Over the next twenty-five years, this land would be developed by the college into the Tuck Mall/Tuck Drive area of the campus.

In spite of the expansion programs of Presidents Tucker and Nichols, the biggest building and re-development boom that the college would experience came under the longtime direction of President Ernest Martin Hopkins (1916–1945). Here was a methodically far-reaching man who not only had a clear vision of Dartmouth's future but knew how to raise the necessary funds to sustain that vision. With Hanover architect Jens Fredrik Larson at his side, Hopkins erected twenty-six major new buildings about the campus—designed in the timeless Georgian style so favored by Mr. Hopkins' generation.

Hanover and Dartmouth were to experience the same pains as the rest of the country during this fifty-year period, for the peace and tranquil beauty of the place were not buffers against the agonies of two world wars and the Great Depression. However, despite the social and economic upheavals of the first half of the twentieth century, the village and college continued to evolve, becoming eventually the special place that so many cherish today, more than fifty years later.

The material presented within the pages of this book is arranged as a sort of walking tour, starting on the Vermont side of the Connecticut River at the Hanover-Norwich railroad station—where so many people arrived and first saw the community fifty to one hundred years ago. The reader then travels up to Main Street where the village and college are visited as though on foot. While it is not possible to show every building or vista of the period, it is hoped that the flavor of the community will soon emerge and provide the reader with hours of enjoyable study.

One
From the Depot up
to Main Street

October 1848 saw the opening of the Connecticut & Passumpsic Rivers Railroad up the valley as far as Bradford, Vermont. Until the closing of the depot located immediately across the river in Lewiston on December 1, 1959, this was Hanover and Dartmouth's vital link to the outside world. By the turn of the century, tons of freight and thousands of students and visitors to the village arrived and departed here yearly via the Boston & Maine Railroad.

The second bridge crossing the Connecticut River was built at this site in 1796. The much-admired Ledyard Bridge, the fourth span at this location, was a marvel of wooden engineering completed in 1859. This view looks north about 1915.

A turn-of-the-century horse-drawn buggy is beginning the climb up to Main Street, having just come across Ledyard Bridge from the depot. Starting in 1909, sections of the hill were graded and paved; however, it would be at least a decade before the work was complete. Until then, the road alternated between a dust bowl and a muddy quagmire.

In spite of attempts to strengthen the wooden bridge in the spring of 1927, its replacement was becoming imminent. In late 1934, a temporary single-lane span was erected immediately south of the old structure, and the beloved Ledyard Bridge was dismantled, its timbers salvaged for re-use elsewhere around the valley.

Designed by the State of New Hampshire and constructed as a WPA project like many public works during the 1930s, the new Ledyard Bridge was completed in late 1935. The graceful steel and concrete structure ended up costing a total of $153,000—$28,000 over budget!

Prior to the construction of flood control dams along the major tributaries of the Connecticut River in the 1940s and 1950s, destructive flooding was always a worry, as this view attests. Here the high waters of the famous November 1927 flood are surging under the elderly wooden covered bridge. In the background is Lewiston, Vermont.

Before the advent of mechanical refrigeration in the 1920s, the river furnished ice for the village and campus area. The blocks of harvested ice would be packed into sawdust within specially designed buildings called ice houses; then, during warmer months, they were distributed into individual ice boxes.

Beginning in the late nineteenth century, the Connecticut River saw many annual spring log drives. By about 1910, they reached their zenith—sometimes floating as much as sixty-five million feet of logs from northern New Hampshire and Vermont south to saw and paper mills in Massachusetts. This view shows the 1912 spring drive passing under Ledyard Bridge.

And sometimes log jams did occur! The river men hated Ledyard Bridge with its large center masonry pier situated at a narrow place on the great stream. This situation often caused large jams to pick up behind it, as seen here opposite the site of Dartmouth College's present boathouse facility, c. 1910.

Accompanying the log drives were rafts, also made of logs, that carried workhorses—used in the woods during the winter—downstream in case they were needed to untangle a jam. Other rafts, commonly referred to as "Mary Anns," carried the cooks' shanties. This view was taken from Ledyard Bridge looking upstream c. 1910.

Here a log-driving crew breaks for dinner along the shore near Ledyard Bridge. A careful inspection of this c. 1910 photograph will reveal the spikes imbedded in the bottoms of the men's shoes, which allowed them to stay afoot on the wet logs.

Looking from the bluff around 1900 at what is now Sargent Street, Ledyard Bridge and the river are visible at the base of the hill. The village of Lewiston, Vermont, is beyond. The sloping bank to the immediate left is the bluff at the end of Downing Road.

This *c.* 1910 photograph, taken about halfway up West Wheelock Street toward the river and looking south, shows the back of the old Hanover High School building, once located on Allen Street. An addition to the rear of the building had been completed in 1896 at a cost of $6,988.91.

After reaching the top of Wheelock Street heading towards the village center, this early-twentieth-century view looks back westerly into the hills of Vermont. It was only during this time that West Wheelock Street came to be called by its present name—prior to then it was commonly referred to as "River Hill."

Looking from the brow of the hill up the last stretch of West Wheelock Street towards its intersection with Main Street, this *c.* 1910 view shows the south side of the street starting at School Street on the far right. The first building is the Phi Gamma Delta fraternity house at 10 West Wheelock Street.

Built about 1840 by Mrs. A.A. Brewster as a residence for her son, the home was actually made up of an old barn and house moved from the opposite side of School Street. In 1903, the Greek-pillared facade was added from material salvaged when Cobb's Store was torn down on South Main Street to make way for the second half of the Davison Building. The property became the Phi Gamma Delta fraternity house in 1907.

In 1936 the fraternity decided to replace the old wood-framed house and to construct in its place a new and larger brick building. Designed in the Georgian Revival style by Chicago architect Alfred Hoyt Granger, the new facility was dedicated in December 1937.

Until it was torn down in 1971, this was the oldest structure surviving in the village, and the first two-story building to have been constructed here. Erected in 1771 on the corner of South Main and West Wheelock Streets, in front of the present Casque & Gauntlet House, it was first used as a tavern. Moved to its West Wheelock Street site in 1823, the building remained a private residence until purchased by the Delta Kappa Epsilon fraternity in 1908; they added the Greek Revival trim and portico, and an addition to the rear of the house. This photograph was taken c. 1915.

Erected in 1773 as the residence of Eleazar Wheelock, founder of Dartmouth College, this building originally had a gambrel roof and was located on the present site of Reed Hall, facing the green. It was moved to West Wheelock Street in 1838, and the roofline was altered in 1846. In 1900 the Howe family donated their home for use as the village library. The Colonial Revival portico and other trim were added in 1900, and the brick stacks in 1912 (this photograph was taken c. 1925). The building served nobly as a library until a new facility was constructed in 1975 on the other side of the village.

About 1827, Elam Markham constructed his residence on the brow of River Hill. Until it was purchased by the Theta Delta Chi fraternity in 1908, it remained a private home occupied by an interesting variety of individuals. The fraternity substantially remodeled the house in 1909 and made additions to it as well. In 1924, a fire seriously damaged the structure, forcing its demolition and replacement a year later.

Delta Chi's new fraternity house was designed by the architectural firm of Putnam and Chandler of Boston, Massachusetts, and dedicated in the fall of 1926. It is an excellent building in the Colonial Revival style with fine Georgian detailing.

Designed by the well-known New York City architect Frederick Clarke Withers, St. Thomas Episcopal Church took two years to complete due to a chronic shortage of funds. When finished in 1876, the church construction had cost parishioners upwards of $50,000. A planned 150-foot stone tower was never even built. However, a stone narthex and cloister designed by Hanover architect Frank J. Barrett Sr. were added to the west end in 1959. St. Thomas Church, designed in the Gothic Revival style, is considered by architectural historians to be Mr. Withers' finest work.

Several different buildings occupied this lot and numerous uses were made of this land before the Psi Upsilon fraternity erected their new house here at 7 West Wheelock Street in 1907. The house was designed in the Craftsman style, in stark contrast to other fraternity houses around the village area. An addition was constructed to the building about 1940 (this photograph was taken c. 1915).

20

Dr. Samuel Alden constructed this impressive brick residence—seen here *c.* 1910—at the southwest corner of South Main and West Wheelock Streets in 1823; since 1893, the structure has been the home of the Casque and Gauntlet Society. In 1915, the old brick-backed, one-and-a-half-story ell was replaced by a larger brick addition, and other modifications were executed as well, all under the direction of architect Fred Wentworth, Dartmouth Class of 1886 and past member of the Casque and Gauntlet, a school honor society. The building is one of the few Federal style buildings remaining in Hanover.

H.T. Howe's horse-drawn bus has just rounded the corner from West Wheelock onto South Main Street, bringing passengers up from the depot in this *c.* 1910 view. In the background is the Casque and Gauntlet House. Mr. Hamilton T. "Hamp" Howe's livery stable was located on Allen Street and was one of four in the village. In addition to service provided by the village's livery stables, there were also three other independent stages that met the daily trains at Lewiston in a fiercely competitive and active business.

This view is of the third structure on this corner since 1782 to be utilized as an inn. Erected in 1888 from the design of well-known St. Johnsbury, Vermont, architect Lambert Packard, the building cost $22,500 and for the first time was under the college's ownership. Because of poor planning and faulty workmanship, in 1902 the facility was extensively remodeled at a cost of $58,000, making what had been a rather flamboyant Victorian building a little bit more Colonial Revival in appearance. During the summer of 1966, this building succumbed to the wrecker's ball, making way for the present inn.

Since 1771 when the "village at the college" was laid out largely under the direction of Hanover pioneer Jonathan Freeman, the intersection of Main and Wheelock Streets has always been considered the center of the community. This c. 1910 view looks from the front of Dartmouth's new College Hall south down Main Street. The Hanover Inn sits majestically on its corner, and visible in front of the inn on the left is the community's horse-watering trough—a solid piece of stone set in the shade providing refreshment to both horses and an occasional village dog.

Two

Main Street and around the Village

This late 1920s view looks south down Main Street from just north of the "Inn Corner." Gone is the horse-watering trough that for many years was located at the corner to the left. The street was first partially paved in 1901, the same year the first automobile was observed operating in the village. Other village improvements of this era included the following: gas street lights (1875), electric street lights (1893), and the first telephone exchange with twenty-six subscribers (1901). The first telephone in the village, located in the Dartmouth Bookstore, appeared more than ten years before the exchange was established.

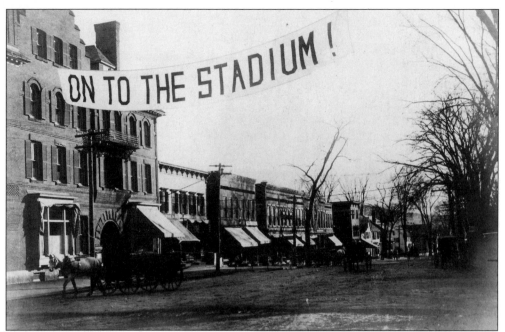

Judging from the banner stretched across South Main Street in this *c.* 1905 view, the Dartmouth football team must be preparing to meet an arch rival out on the gridiron at the stadium. Maybe Harvard is in town! To the immediate left is the recently remodeled Hanover Inn.

The lobby of the Hanover Inn *c.* 1910 looks as fashionable and comfortable as any building interior within the village.

The Cobb's Store Building—originally built in 1793 by Rufus Graves and later remodeled about ten years with Greek Revival pillars to look as it appears here—will be torn down in 1903 to make way for the second half of the Davison Block (the first half was constructed in 1893), visible in the center of the photograph. The large Bridgman Block to the left of Frank W. Davison's building was erected by Don S. Bridgman in 1900, replacing three old wood-framed structures.

The Bridgman, Davison, and Cobb's Store Buildings are decked out for the Fourth of July, about 1902.

During the night of October 30, 1906, the six-year-old Bridgman Building completely burned, leaving by morning a blackened brick shell and $30,000 of damage. Only because of determined efforts by firefighters was the blaze kept to only this structure.

A new Bridgman Building was erected in 1907 by Don S. Bridgman. Designed by Louis Sheldon Newton, an architect from Hartford, Vermont, the building replaced the block that burned the previous fall. This is believed to be a builder's photograph, taken shortly after construction was completed.

This late 1940s view looks down South Main Street after a fresh snowfall. The most recent block to be constructed on the street is the Lang Building, built in 1937 and designed by Jens Fredrik Larson. The building stands beside the Hanover Inn in the left foreground. To the right is the Davison Building.

Until well into the 1950s, snow removal on Main Street was typically done by hand, as this photograph taken about 1950 shows.

Looking north up the west side of South Main Street about 1910, we see two wood-framed buildings in the foreground that would give way to the ravages of fire in 1914 and 1929 respectively. The furthest building to the left housed the printing presses of Frank A. Musgrove, and is today the site of the Musgrove Building; the structure in the center of this view housed the village precinct offices, the police station, and fire apparatus. Allen Street runs between them, and to the far right is the Bridgman Block.

Constructed by John Young c. 1780, in later years this building came to be known as the "Walker House" and was purchased by the village precinct in 1906 to house municipal offices, a meeting space, the police station, and a firehouse. A minor fire in the attic occurred in 1918; however, the village's new fire engine had only to travel from the rear of the building to extinguish it. The building was sold in early 1929 to George Gitsis for $40,100. Gitsis ran his campus cafe here until the building completely burned less than a year later. Allen Street is to the left and today the Dartmouth Bookstore occupies the site.

Built about 1820 by Abraham Dunklee, this Main Street building was for many years known as the "Huntington House" for its longtime inhabitant, Newton S. Huntington. Like many of the original residences fronting on the street, it eventually evolved into a place of business. In 1899, young Frank A. Musgrove purchased the building to house his Dartmouth Press, which published the *Hanover Gazette*. On the night of May 3, 1914, the old building burned and was soon replaced by the present Musgrove Block.

Frank A. Musgrove's new business block was completed in 1915. For sixteen years until the construction of their own facility on the corner of Lebanon and South Main Streets, the post office occupied the northern half of the first floor, and Mr. Musgrove's Dartmouth Press was in the adjoining half.

For many years, Allen Street was home to at least one of the village's livery stables, a large enterprise run by the colorful Ira Babcock Allen. Later the business passed to Hamilton T. "Hamp" Howe, who renamed it the Inn Stables, with reference to the stage and livery service that he provided the Hanover Inn. By the early 1920s, owners Charles Nash and Frank Tenney recognized that the automobile was here to stay, and in 1922 erected this new building to service and store the vehicles. Today this same structure at 5 Allen Street houses EBA's restaurant and the Dartmouth Bookstore.

In 1946, Ray Buskey, owner of the Inn Garage, had taken on selling the new line of Kaiser-Frazer automobiles. Using the building at 5 Allen Street as a showroom, Buskey renovated this complex of old wooden buildings at 7 Allen Street to provide much-needed service space. These structures were demolished in 1978 to make way for the present three-story commercial block.

This early 1910s view of the east side of South Main Street shows the Hanover Inn at the corner facing the green. The middle two structures for many years housed Campion's Clothing Store and A.W. Guyer's grocery store until both burned on February 8, 1937, and were replaced later that year by the present Lang Building. All four of these buildings were built in 1888 following the aftermath of the great fire of January 4, 1887.

Following the destructive fire of 1887, the east side of South Main Street was fully rebuilt within a year. Longtime Hanover resident John L. Bridgman constructed the two-story block in the immediate right foreground; fellow well-known businessman Dorrance B. Currier built the companion block adjacent to it. For many years the post office was a tenant in the space today occupied by McLaughry Associates Realtors.

American Express and rival Railway Express both had offices on Main Street that did a brisk business delivering freight to and from the Boston & Maine Railroad station in Lewiston. By the 1920s, the delivery horses seen in this c. 1910 view gave way to motorized trucks; however, Railway Express would keep an office on Main Street until the early 1950s.

The house in the center of this view, which was built about 1780, originally stood on the site of the Hanover Inn and was the first such building at that location to serve as a tavern. Moved to the corner of South Main and Lebanon Streets in 1813, it was a residence for one hundred years until it was torn down in 1913 to make way for the new Dartmouth Savings Bank Building.

Like many storefronts on business blocks across the country during the 1930s and early 1940s, the front of the Bridgman Building on the east side of South Main Street got a stylish new facelift. What had been L.B. Downing's Drug Store became Putnam's following Mr. Downing's death in 1918. Today the space is occupied by Pizzazz and McLaughry Associates Realtors.

One of the Tanzi brothers is taking inventory of fruit on display in front of the brothers' South Main Street store. Immediately beyond is Eastman's Drug Store, located in an old wood-framed building that was demolished in 1959 to make way for the expansion of the Dartmouth Savings Bank Building.

From 1897 until their retirement on June 30, 1969, the Tanzi family operated a fruit and grocery store from this modest wood-framed building halfway down the east side of South Main Street. This early turn-of-the-century view shows the building perhaps several years after Angelo Tanzi's purchase of the property. The building burned in December 1975.

The village's first piece of motorized fire-fighting equipment was purchased for $1,500 in 1915. In 1928, the village precinct erected a new firehouse and municipal building to house the growing fleet of fire trucks. The new facility was designed by Hanover architects Larson & Wells and cost $50,611.09, not including land costs. This view was taken in 1949 and shows the village's latest piece of equipment—a 1948 Maxim pumper recently purchased for $14,500.

The first building constructed in the village specifically as a bank stood on the present site of Robinson Hall, facing the green. Erected in 1870, it functioned well until the completion of this building in 1913 at the corner of South Main and Lebanon Streets. Even after the facility was substantially enlarged in 1959, its common lobby served both the Dartmouth Savings and Dartmouth National Banks until 1975, although the savings bank owned the property.

This handsome brick residence for many years occupied the corner of Lebanon and South Main Streets, now the site of the post office. Constructed about 1836 by Major William Tenney, a blacksmith, it came into the possession of the Storrs family in 1883 and remained so until the property's sale to the federal government in 1928. The following year, the home was razed. Beyond is the Heneage House, demolished in 1964 to allow further expansion of the post office.

This photograph was taken for the federal government in the fall of 1930 to record work started on the new post office building. Looking from the rear of the property and westerly toward South Main Street, we see the old Fairfield Block to the right, demolished in 1969 and today the site of the Nugget Arcade Building, and two residences demolished in 1950 to make way for the Nugget Theater. To the left is the Tavern Block.

The village's new post office facility was constructed by W.H. Trumbull of Hanover and completed in April 1931. Lebanon also received a new post office building about this same time, and legend has it that the final locations of the two buildings mistakenly got switched due to incorrect labeling of the architectural drawings in far-off Washington, D.C.!

In 1894, one of the village's more colorful entrepreneurs, Dorrance B. Currier, erected this structure that came to be called the "Tavern Block" with reference to a restaurant located on the lower story. The building provided lodging upstairs and served other commercial uses. By 1957, the building had become run-down and was demolished to make way for a municipal parking lot. Today the Fleet Building occupies this spot on the corner of South Main and Maple Streets.

A hunting party consisting of several Main Street merchants proudly shows off their game in front of the Tavern Block, c. 1905.

The Great Atlantic & Pacific Tea Company, more commonly referred to simply as the "A&P," was one of the nation's first large retailers of food, and early on it maintained a presence in the village within the Tavern Block. Here the staff, complete with delivery horse, is assembled for a promotional photograph, *c.* 1910.

In 1935, Gulf Oil Corporation purchased the residence of Miss Nellie Newton and in its place constructed this large service station and garage facility on the corner of South Main and Maple Streets. Operated for many years by the Manchester family, this structure was replaced in 1963 by the building presently home to the Food Stop. This view was taken shortly before the 1935 building was demolished.

This view looks up South Main Street, *c.* 1905, from the brow of the hill heading down to Mink Brook. On the immediate right is the building still existing at 72 South Main Street and presently housing the Buon Gustaio Restaurant. Upon close inspection, one can see the recently constructed Tavern Block on the left and through the trees.

Looking south from the end of Main Street at the top of "Benton Hill," as it was then known, the village area ends, and there are only farms until the next community of West Lebanon. Starting in the early 1920s, residential development began to take place along both sides of the road. In 1940, the entire road to the town line was rebuilt and straightened out, eliminating several dangerous curves.

The bridge over Mink Brook at the base of South Main Street, or West Lebanon Road as it was commonly called, was for years a source of ongoing troublesome maintenance. Finally, during the summer of 1914, the Town of Hanover erected a new stone structure, shown under construction in this postcard view.

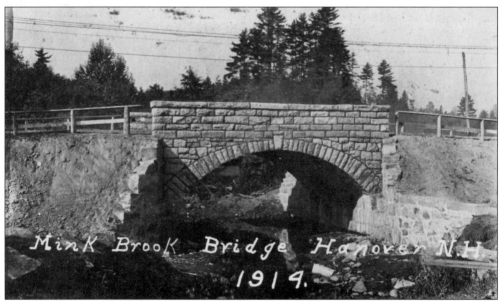

So proud was the community of their new bridge that upon completion a second postcard view was published. Built with granite foundation blocks that were free for the taking from the old bank building then being demolished on North Main Street, the bridge served the village well for twenty-six years until being demolished when the road was relocated in 1940.

This construction photograph of the post office site was taken during the summer of 1930. Looking from South Main Street across to Lebanon Street, the view shows hand laborers digging the foundations and basement of the new facility. In the center background are a series of wood-framed residences razed in 1959 for the construction of Hopkins Center. The Dartmouth Savings Bank Building is just out of view to the left of the photograph. The two-story white house to the right at 3 Lebanon Street was demolished in 1968, and today the site is occupied by the front portion of the Hanover Park Building.

The village's last riding and livery stable is shown next to Hanover's first diner in this mid-1920s view. Bachand's operation would soon close, a victim of the automobile, while the diner would remain until being removed in 1962. Today, the Hanover Park Building on Lebanon Street and a parking lot occupy the site.

The rear portion of this building located on the northeast corner of South College and Lebanon Streets was originally built in 1840 as a Methodist church. The Episcopalians obtained the property in 1850 and sold it in 1872 to the Kibling family, who first used it for an opera house. In 1887 they added the three-story front building and transformed the structure into a hotel. Acquired by Dartmouth College in 1922, it was used as a dormitory known as South Hall until it was torn down in 1959.

Rogers Garage was already a well-established Packard and Chevrolet dealership when this showroom addition was constructed in 1931. Designed by Wells & Hudson architects of Hanover, this was a Lebanon Street landmark until it was torn down in 1966. To the left in this 1956 view is the rear of South Hall, and to the left rear is the college's heating plant smokestack.

Designed by the Hanover architectural firm of Larson & Wells in 1922, a new Roman Catholic church located on Lebanon Street was begun in the spring of 1923. Mass was celebrated there for the first time in November 1924. The building was constructed on land that up until 1918 was part of Dorrance B. Currier's large village farm.

When Sanborn Road first opened for development in 1906, it fronted on the wide-open pastures of Dorrance B. Currier's 150-acre farm, which included most of the area immediately south of the village. These turn-of-the-century homes along Sanborn Road were constructed about the time the road was first completed.

After much study and debate, the village finally decided to construct a new grade school out on old pastureland recently annexed to the Currier farm. Built in 1924 at a cost of $98,500, the new structure was designed by Hanover architects Larson & Wells and constructed by W.H. Trumbull, also of Hanover.

By the early 1930s, it became apparent that the village also required a new high school. A new building costing $203,849 was designed by Wells, Hudson & Granger of Hanover and erected in 1935 immediately south of the recent grade school. The first class graduated in June 1937 from this impressive state-of-the-art facility.

In 1931, Shell Oil Company constructed this modest wood-framed service station at the intersection of Lebanon and South Park Streets. By 1954, a larger brick facility replaced this first building, and in 1994 Ledyard National Bank erected a drive-up branch bank on the site.

By 1937, the Socony Oil Company also constructed a service station at the end of South Park Street to compete with Shell's facility. This early automotive service building was likewise demolished and replaced c. 1950; about twenty years later, it was replaced again with the present Co-op Service Center facility.

Looking north up the east side of School Street about 1905, in the foreground is a residence built about 1816 by Lemuel Davenport, with porches added later in the nineteenth century. Today, the building is the Rectory of St. Thomas Episcopal Church. Beyond is the residence of William Avery, which was constructed in 1868 and today is the recreation center for the Town of Hanover.

Originally constructed by G.C. Furber in 1898 as his residence at 8 School Street, this building became the home of the Delta Tau Delta fraternity during the first decade of the twentieth century. More recently, the building has been a small apartment house. The mansard-roofed structure beyond is the old Ashbel Hotel, torn down in 1973—today the site of a municipal parking lot.

After years of bickering amongst the village's citizens, the subject of a new schoolhouse at last came to a favorable conclusion in 1877 with the construction of this facility on Allen Street. Designed by Dartmouth Professor Frank A. Sherman, the new building was constructed by Mead, Mason and Company of Lebanon at a total cost of $10,933.04. An addition was placed on the rear of the building in 1896. This view was taken in 1917 looking northeast.

Growing school enrollment required that the village construct this new high school building in 1912 on the south side of Allen Street, across from the 1877 facility. Designed by Boston architect E.J. Wilson, and constructed by J.H. Davidson of the same city, the new facility cost $30,048.50. Both buildings were sold in 1936 for $3,000 and torn down after the construction of a new high school on Lebanon Street.

What prompted Lucien B. Downing to publish this *c.* 1905 postcard view of himself and his wife, Martha Downing, in front of their 19 Allen Street home is no longer known. Born in Hartford, Vermont, "Deacon" Downing—as he was familiarly known for many years—owned and operated L.B. Downing's Drug Store at 36 South Main Street until his death in 1918.

The years surrounding the turn of the century comprised a wonderful period of domestic architecture for this country, and the village saw the construction of some delightful shingled residences at this time. This home at 30 Maple Street is a wonderful example. It was designed by architect Louis Sheldon Newton, of Hartford, Vermont, and constructed in 1909 for Charles Nash, who owned the livery stable on Allen Street. Today, it is the residence of the Tefft family.

Three

Around the Dartmouth Green

DARTMOUTH COLLEGE

The above bird's-eye view is a very accurate artist's rendition of the campus in 1906. Gradually, the old is giving way to the new, as the newer buildings scattered around the green attest.

College Hall, Dartmouth College, Hanover, N. H.

During the night of February 8, 1900, the large, ornate Second Empire style Victorian building known as the "Golden Corner" burned beyond repair. Later in the year, the college bought the property, cleared away the rubble of the burned twenty-five-year-old building, and erected College Hall (shown in this view taken shortly after the building's completion in 1901). Beyond we see the Dartmouth Savings Bank Building.

The new College Hall was designed by architect Charles A. Rich and cost $119,382. The building was originally designed as a multi-purpose facility with dormitory rooms, a living room, administrative offices, and a dining hall seating four hundred students with full kitchen facilities in the basement. This early view of the living room illustrates the height of period fashion.

50

Before the time when the village's streets were cleared of snow so as to accommodate automobiles, "ski-joring" was an occasional student pastime, as illustrated above. With the fresh snow rolled to allow sleigh travel, all a student needed was a horse or two, skies, and a harness. In the background of this *c.* 1910 photograph is the green, Wentworth Street, and Webster Hall.

This late 1920s view looking up north Main Street from the Hanover Inn corner shows the street built out to its present-day appearance; we have, however, lost many of the campus's elm trees over the years. This section of North Main Street was first paved in 1907 at an expense of $1,845, changing an occasional mud hole into a gracious boulevard.

Commonly known for many years as Sanborn Hall, the front portion of this building was erected in 1819 as the residence of Dr. Cyrus Perkins. Owned and sold several times by the college through the nineteenth century, the structure was converted in 1894 into a dormitory with $20,861 in improvements. It was the first residential facility on campus with flush toilets. The old Dartmouth Savings Bank Building is visible at the left.

In 1913, Sanborn Hall was moved back, the old Dartmouth Savings Bank Building was demolished, and Robinson Hall was constructed. Designed by Charles A. Rich, the new building cost $192,000 and was the gift of Wallace F. Robinson, a businessman from Reading, Vermont, who never attended Dartmouth but had a brother in the Class of 1851. Mr. Robinson specified that the stylish Neoclassical building must only be used by undergraduate students for artistic and intellectual activities.

Like Sanborn Hall originally beside it, Proctor House—as it was for many years called—also faced the green until it was moved back in 1902. Constructed by Professor Ebenezer Adams in 1810 utilizing an older building for a back ell, the property was acquired by the college in 1902 as a site for Tuck Hall, today known as McNutt Hall. After being moved back from the green to its new location shown here, the building was demolished in 1912 to make way for South Massachusetts Hall.

About 1784, Samuel McClure built this residence on the present-day site of Parkhurst Hall. Dr. Shurtleff purchased the property in 1807, and it remained in his family's possession until the death of his daughter, Mrs. Susan A. Brown, in 1900. At that time, it was acquired by the college and torn down in 1910 to make way for Parkhurst Hall.

In August 1901, Edward Tuck, Class of 1862, gave the college $135,000 worth of stock to fund the "erecting, equipping, and maintaining a building suited to the uses of the Tuck School of Administration and Finance." Mr. Tuck, a multi-millionaire banker living in Paris, had established the graduate school two years earlier, naming it for his father, Amos Tuck. The new building, designed in the popular Neoclassical style by Charles A. Rich, was erected in 1902 and cost $125,000. It was dedicated in 1904 and named Tuck Hall.

After the Tuck School moved to its new quarters down on Tuck Mall in 1930, the old building was extensively remodeled. Spending $112,000 of $366,000 received from Randolph McNutt, Class of 1871, college architect Jens Fredrik Larson added a third floor and gave the building much more of a Georgian appearance. Upon completion, the building was renamed McNutt Hall in honor of its most recent benefactor.

Professor Oliver P. Hubbard constructed the brick residence shown on the right in the this 1842 photograph. Late in the century, the building was acquired by the college, and in 1899, $11,923 was spent to remodel it into a twenty-student dormitory. In 1910, the building was demolished to make way for the construction of Parkhurst Hall. In the background is Hubbard Hall No. 2 (see also Chapter 4).

Named for and given in honor of Wilder L. Parkhurst, Parkhurst Hall was part of a $178,000 gift from Lewis Parkhurst, Class of 1878, to commemorate the death of his son during his freshman year at Dartmouth. Designed as an administration building by Charles A. Rich, the new facility cost $118,000 and was dedicated in 1911. Both the Shurtleff House and Hubbard Hall were demolished to make space for Parkhurst's construction.

THE WHITE CHAPEL. DARTMOUTH COLLEGE. HANOVER N.H.

Officially known as the Church of Christ at Dartmouth College, for 136 years until its destruction by fire in 1931, this New England meetinghouse kept watch over the green. Erected in 1795 at a cost of $5,000, the meetinghouse received numerous alterations over the years, the most notable by the famous New York architect Stanford White in 1889.

Wentworth Street is shown here c. 1895. Choate House, the closest to the viewer of these three wood-framed dwellings, was one of the many buildings moved to make way for the construction of Baker Library. Erected in 1786 by Reverend Sylvanus Ripley, the building was relocated to North Main Street in 1927. In 1963, Choate House was once again moved further up the same street.

Like its companion adjacent to the west, Lord House was in 1920 also moved to make way for a future library building. Erected by William H. Woodard in 1802, the residence was occupied for many years by college President Nathan Lord (1830–1863), hence its name. This excellent period building is thought to have been designed by Joseph Emerson of Norwich, Vermont.

Although the green was first laid out in 1771, it was not until 1831 that the 7.5-acre college-owned parcel was graded and seeded. Prior to that time, it was a somewhat marshy area of stumps and irregular terrain that drained to the southeast corner, and the road to Lyme cut diagonally across it. This view taken in 1898, three years before the start of construction of Webster Hall, looks northeast towards Rollins Chapel.

Because of Baker Library's completion in 1928 and the church's destruction by fire in 1931, this view was only possible for about three years. The small Greek Revival vestry building beside the church was built in 1841, and together with the larger church structure, they were often referred to as "the cow and the calf."

President Hopkins had hoped to move the old White Church and get it out from in front of the new Baker Library. Also, he wanted to relocate it to the site occupied by the then out-of-style Rollins Chapel. No one of that generation believed that demolishing that pile of "Victorian rubble" would cause any great architectural loss. However, on the night of May 13, 1931, the White Church took fire in a spectacular blaze that originated in a basement trashcan. The sky was lit up and could be seen from as far as 40 miles away; the building was totally destroyed.

When George F. Baker asked college President Ernest M. Hopkins in 1924 what could be done with a gift of $25,000, Mr. Hopkins replied, "not much." That conversation marked the first of several gifts from Mr. Baker that would come to total more than one million dollars by 1928 and finance the construction of a memorial to his beloved uncle, Fisher Ames Baker, Class of 1859. Nine buildings were either demolished or moved to make way for this impressive complex, begun in 1926 and dedicated in June of 1928. The final cost was $1,132,000.

The delivery room on the main floor of the library is shown here. Architect Larson's handling of the exquisite Georgian interior detailing was indeed masterful and finely proportioned.

After the cornerstone was laid and the foundations constructed in 1901, work came to a halt on Webster Hall until 1906 when there were sufficient funds on hand to complete the facility. Much of the funding shortage was due to the destruction of Dartmouth Hall in February 1904, and the need to promptly rebuild that important building. When finished in 1907, the impressive new hall designed by Charles A. Rich ended up costing a total of $143,000.

Webster Hall's Neoclassical interior seated fifteen hundred students and for the next fifty-five years, until the completion of Hopkins Center in 1962, was the college's only large auditorium. Convocation, commencement, town meetings, and voting for the village all took place here—the hall even served as a movie house for seven years when the community lost the first Nugget Theatre in 1944.

The Rollins family originally planned to construct Rollins Chapel of marble; however, cost dictated the use of Lebanon pink granite with Longmeadow sandstone trim instead. Constructed in 1884 at a cost of $32,000 from plans prepared by architect John Lyman Faxon of Boston, the compactness and much of the excellence of the original design were lost with expansion of the apse in 1908 and the extension of the two transepts in 1912. The building is named for the parents of Edward A. Rollins, Class of 1851, an early benefactor to the college.

This *c.* 1915 view of Wentworth, Dartmouth, and Thornton Halls portrays an atmosphere known and loved by thousands world-wide—one of quiet dignity and timeless beauty.

Wentworth Hall was constructed as a pair with its twin, Thornton Hall, in 1829. Designed by architect Ammi B. Young, the two buildings each measured 70-by-50 feet and cost a total of about $12,000. Wentworth Hall was named for John Wentworth II, New Hampshire's last colonial governor and an early benefactor of the college. The hall was extensively remodeled in 1912 at an expense of $40,000.

The first Dartmouth Hall, constructed over a seven-year period and finished in 1791, is thought to be the design of noted colonial New England architect Peter Harrison. Originally, the college planned to construct the hall of brick, but severe budget constraints instead dictated a wood building measuring 150-by-50 feet, at a final cost of about $15,000. For many years, Dartmouth Hall was the college—and also the largest academic building in all New England.

On the morning of February 18, 1904, while the students were in the chapel and the temperature was twenty degrees below zero, a fire that resulted from faulty electrical wiring started in the roof under the belfry, and the first Dartmouth Hall was quickly and completely razed by a spectacular blaze. Although there were no human injuries, the loss of the beloved old building was traumatic and sent shock waves through the Dartmouth alumni community across the nation.

The new Dartmouth Hall, dedicated February 17, 1906, was almost a duplicate of the original building, only 6 feet wider and this time constructed of brick as Eleazar Wheelock had originally wished. Reconstructed by college architect Charles A. Rich, the new building cost $101,700 and is named for William Legge, Second Earl of Dartmouth—the college's sponsor to King George III in 1769 and for whom the college is also named.

Thornton Hall, erected in 1829 as a companion to Wentworth Hall, was named for John Thornton, a wealthy London merchant and philanthropist who admired and believed in Eleazar Wheelock's work of educating Native Americans. When the college was in its infancy, Thornton's numerous monetary gifts were essential to keeping the school going. In 1924, the whole interior area of the building was entirely reconstructed at a cost of $66,000.

Since 1834, the college had been appealing for funds to construct an urgently needed fourth building, but the plea went unfulfilled until the Honorable William Reed of Marblehead, Massachusetts, died in February 1837 and left $19,500 to the college in his will. A self-made man of mercantile pursuits, Mr. Reed was a judge, a Congressman from the Bay State, and a Dartmouth College trustee.

Like Wentworth and Thornton Halls, Reed Hall was designed by architect Ammi B. Young and is a masterpiece of Greek Revival architecture applied with subtlety and dignity. The brick 100-by-50-foot building was erected in 1839 after the old Wheelock Mansion was removed from the site, and the hall was dedicated the following year. Ammi Young would go on to have a distinguished career as a nationally well-known architect. This c. 1905 postcard is clearly mislabeled.

Master plans do not always work out. A fourth building matching Reed Hall was planned for the site later occupied in 1884 by Rollins Chapel. However, a severe economic depression in the late 1930s and changing architectural tastes, which turned against the Greek Revival style and its crisp symmetry, resulted in other plans being made following the Civil War.

This view features the Neoclassical Revival facade of Charles A. Rich's Webster Hall, and its massive Corinthian columns.

The Colonial Revival front of Dartmouth Hall, as reconstructed in 1904 by Charles A. Rich, is shown here.

Although the college acquired the site in 1872 for a future library, it was not until 1884 that Wilson Hall, designed by Boston architect Samuel J.T. Thayer as a 130,000-volume library, was erected. Named in honor of George F. Wilson of western Massachusetts as a result of his $50,000 bequest to the college, the final cost of the building in 1885 was $66,622.32. Curiously, Mr. Wilson never attended Dartmouth.

Perhaps one of the more curious buildings erected on campus during the post-Civil War period was Bissell Hall. Constructed in 1867 as the college's first gymnasium, it was the gift of wealthy New York lawyer George A. Bissell, Class of 1845. The Italianate building was designed by architect Joseph R. Richards of the Boston firm of Richards and Park and cost $23,850. Mr. Bissell made his fortune as one of the first persons to recognize the commercial value of petroleum. In 1959, the building was demolished to make way for the Hopkins Center, and today, the "Top-of-the-Hop" occupies the site.

Prior to the start of the construction of Hopkins Center in 1959, College Street was a small connection between Wheelock and Lebanon Streets featuring a wide variety of buildings, such as the Dragon Tomb. Located next to Wilson Hall, this building was originally built in 1860 by the Kappa Kappa Kappa Society. In 1917, the Dragon Society remodeled the structure, adding the Greek colonnaded front, entablature, and pediment gable.

The campus side of the Hanover Inn was photographed about 1905. Prior to the extensive renovation of the facility that was completed in 1902, this facade had multi-storied porches across its full width, allowing guests an unparalleled view of the green.

In 1924, a large addition was constructed on the east side of the Hanover Inn. Designed by Jens Fredrik Larson, the new wing contained kitchen and dining rooms, as well as additional guest suites, and cost $204,000. This portion of the building still stands, although the original building was replaced in 1966.

The comfortable front porch of the Hanover Inn c. 1925 was a wonderful vantage point from which to study the green and keep an eye on the "Inn Corner"—the site of the perpetual pageant of Hanover village life.

Until the construction of Hopkins Center in 1959, the area east of the Hanover Inn and behind Bissell Hall was a lush garden oasis known as the Inn Gardens. Early in this century, the area had an indoor wooden running track set up that had been part of Bissell Hall when that building was a gymnasium.

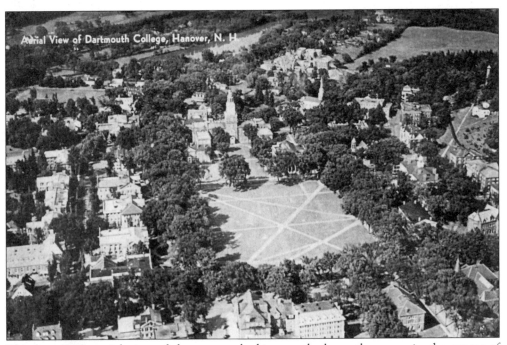

This late 1940s aerial view of the campus looking north shows the green in the center of the photograph.

Four

The West Side
of the Campus

THE BETA THETA PI HOUSE. DARTHMOUTH COLLEGE. HANOVER N.H.

This Colonial Revival-style building built in 1890 was for many years the home of the Beta Theta Pi fraternity. The structure still stands today on its original site at the end of Sanborn Lane and now is known as South Fairbanks. In 1963, the northern half was added—having been moved from a location on Elm Street behind Baker Library.

Originally built in 1819 facing the west side of the green, the building received a large addition in 1894, changing the residence into a dormitory for fifty students. In 1913, the whole structure was moved back beside Sanborn Lane to make way for Robinson Hall; finally in 1936, it was demolished to allow for the construction of Thayer Dining Hall.

Thayer Dining Hall was one of the last major buildings constructed on campus during the Hopkins presidency. Designed by Jens Fredrik Larson and completed in 1937, the new facility was named in honor of Henry B. Thayer—a longtime Dartmouth College trustee and close personal friend of President Hopkins.

Hubbard Hall, Dartmouth College. HANOVER, N. H.

Known as Hubbard 2 and located behind the original Hubbard Hall, this forty-eight-student dormitory was erected in 1906 at a cost of $19,804. Four years later in 1910, the building was moved north to allow construction of Parkhurst Hall; finally, in 1931, it was demolished, and the land was utilized as a parking lot. To the left in this *c.* 1915 view is a corner of North Massachusetts Hall.

A group of alumni in Massachusetts proposed to the college trustees that they raise funds throughout the Bay State for a new dormitory. The funds never materialized; however, the trustees named the building Massachusetts Hall regardless. Designed by Charles A. Rich, the new eighty-eight-student dormitory facility was built in 1907 at a cost of $80,000.

South Massachusetts Hall was constructed in 1912 with its twin, North Massachusetts Hall; both were designed by architect Charles A. Rich to flank the original facility completed five years earlier. This 1914 view shows the Class of 1884 in residence for its 30th reunion.

North Massachusetts Hall is shown here while being used by members of the Class of 1889 for their 25th reunion. These two dormitories together cost $152,000 when completed in 1912, and added modern accommodations on campus for 130 more students.

CHANDLER HALL & HUBBARD HOUSE, DARTMOUTH COLLEGE, HANOVER N.H,

Chandler Hall was perhaps the most unfortunate building on the whole campus. First erected in 1837 for Moor's Indian Charity School, the original structure had the simple but eloquent lines of a Greek Revival academy building. However, extensive alterations in 1871 and further alterations and additions in 1898 caused a future generation of Dartmouth men to consider it "unquestionably the ugliest building in Hanover." It was demolished in 1937. To the far right in the photograph is Crosby Hall.

The front portion of Crosby Hall was built in 1810 as a residence for the Reverend Dr. Zephaniah Moore—a professor of Latin and Greek at Dartmouth. Before being acquired by the college in 1884, it was for many years owned by the well-known Dr. Dixi Crosby. In 1896, the original building was extensively altered and a rear addition constructed at a cost of $27,953, providing dormitory space for forty-five students.

75

Hitchcock Hall - Dartmouth College - Hanover N.H.

In 1912, the college acquired the Hitchcock Estate—a 45-acre tract of land extending from North Main Street down to the river. The following year, the first of many buildings was erected on the tract and named in honor of the Hitchcock family. Designed by Charles A. Rich, Hitchcock Hall cost $110,000 and provided residential housing for ninety-two students.

The three dormitory buildings that make up the Gile-Streeter-Lord Hall complex were constructed in 1928 and designed by Jens Fredrik Larson. They cost a total of $505,000, added accommodations for 382 students, and were named for families long prominent in college affairs. Their Georgian Revival architecture adds a quiet dignity and grace to Tuck Mall.

Reverend Henry Fairbanks, a professor at the college, built this Second Empire-style home in 1864, and in the 1870s, he sold the estate to Hiram and Mary Hitchcock of New York City. After acquiring the property in 1912, Dartmouth College briefly used the building until demolishing it in 1920 to make way for Russell Sage Hall. This view shows the old house shortly before it was razed.

Russell Sage Hall, a dormitory built to accommodate 139 students, was completed in 1923 at a cost of $176,000 and designed by Larson & Wells. The new building occupied the site of the old Hitchcock Mansion and was named for Mr. Russell Sage of New York, whose wife's estate bequeathed the college $803,000 in 1918.

Tuck Mall was developed during the 1920s and by late in that decade had assumed the appearance depicted in this *c.* 1928 view. Baker Library had just been completed, and Silsby Hall, visible to the left corner of the mall, was also opened in 1928. The new science building was named in honor of T. Julien Silsby of Brookline, Massachusetts, and his gift of more than $400,000 to the college.

A view taken about 1940 looking down Tuck Drive shows the Tuck School beyond. Much of the beauty of this area of the campus may be attributed to the noted architect John Russell Pope and the master plan that he prepared for the college in 1922.

Since the earliest days of the college, a pathway leading down to the river existed where present-day Tuck Drive passes below tall pine trees. Once known as Webster Vale because it had been the favorite walk of the great expounder during his college days, in later years it was part of the Hitchcock estate.

During the summer of 1914, two years after the college acquired the property, the path down to the river was made more formal with the construction of Tuck Drive—one of many generous gifts of Edward Tuck, also the benefactor of the Tuck School Foundation. The landscape architect for the project was Bremer W. Pond of Boston, Massachusetts.

Almost thirty years after establishing the original Tuck School, Edward Tuck again showed his generosity to the college with a gift of $575,000, which financed the construction of the new Amos Tuck School complex completed in 1930. Designed by Jens Fredrik Larson, the facility was actually four buildings—a central hall, two dormitories, and a refectory.

When completed in September 1939, the Horace S. Cummings Building finally provided the Thayer School of Engineering a permanent home of their own on campus. Prior to this time the school had been holed up in old Bissell Hall—a converted gymnasium. Designed by Jens Fredrik Larson, the new facility was named after an 1862 alumnus and benefactor to the school.

For many years this early home stood on North Main Street at about the present-day west entrance to Baker Library. Erected about 1786 by an otherwise unidentified Thaddeus White, the building was moved in 1925 to 38 East Wheelock Street to allow construction of the new library facility.

Butterfield Hall, through no fault of its own, had a tragically short life. It was erected with the best of intentions in 1895 for the biology, physiology, and geology departments through the generous gift of Dr. Ralph Butterfield of Kansas City, Class of 1839. By 1926, however, the yellow brick Neo-Colonial building designed by Charles A. Rich found itself sitting right where President Hopkins wanted to put a new library. Hence, that year the thirty-one-year-old building was demolished and Baker Library took its place.

The Sanborn English House was named for Edwin David Sanborn, who for nearly fifty years was a professor of English on the campus; the construction was financed by a gift of $1,655,555 from Sanborn's son in 1928. Designed by Jens Fredrik Larson and dedicated in September 1929, the building was supposed to have a twin on the opposite side of Baker Library—a facility for the music department. However, like many master plans, this one never fully materialized.

A gift of $305,000 from Frank P. Carpenter of Manchester, New Hampshire, made possible the Carpenter Fine Arts Building. Similar to the Sanborn English House, the Carpenter Building was designed by architect Jens Fredrik Larson and was also intended to have a twin building opposite Baker Library—this one housing the foreign language department to the northeast. Carpenter Hall was dedicated in June 1929.

This Second Empire-style home was constructed in 1868 by Professor Henry E. Parker, and in 1894, it passed into the possession of the Kappa Kappa Kappa fraternity. Upon completion of the fraternity's new house at 1 Webster Avenue in 1924, the college acquired the property and two years later, demolished the out-of-style Victorian house to make way for the construction of Silsby Hall.

When Reverend Sylvanus Ripley first constructed this home in 1780 on what is now the corner of North Main Street and Webster Avenue, it was considered outside of the village area. Daniel Webster roomed here during his senior year in 1800. In 1928 the building was moved up North Main Street to get it out of the way of Silsby Hall. To the left in the photograph can be seen the Kappa Kappa Kappa fraternity house.

THE CLARK SCHOOL. HANOVER. N. H.

For many years, this house located where the Kiewit Computation Center now stands was home to the Clark School, a boys' college preparatory school that moved in 1954 from Hanover to Canaan, New Hampshire, and became the Cardigan Mountain School. The front house was built about 1833, and it was demolished in 1961 to make room for Kiewit.

CLARK SCHOOL. HANOVER. N. H.

This building was also part of the Clark School. It was built by that institution in 1925, facing the now-gone Elm Street. In 1963, the building was moved over onto Sanborn Lane and attached to the old Beta Theta Pi fraternity house, where today it is known as North Fairbanks.

Joseph L. Dewey constructed this tidy-looking residence for himself in 1842. It came into the possession of E.K. Smith several decades later, much like the property located immediately north (illustrated below). By the 1920s the premises housed the Sigma Nu fraternity. Today, the courtyard of the Kiewit complex occupies the site at 27 North Main Street.

This comfortable mid-nineteenth-century home was erected in 1868 by E.K. Smith, a well-known baker and confectioner who later established a large business in White River Junction, Vermont. Eventually, the building became the home of the Phi Sigma Kappa fraternity until the construction of their new house immediately beside it at 31 North Main Street in 1925, when the old building was demolished.

Kappa Kappa Kappa was the first fraternity to construct a brick, fireproof house on Webster Avenue during the 1920s. Erected in 1924, the building is a superb example of the Colonial Revival style so popular during the early decades of the twentieth century.

Like so many of the fraternities on campus during the 1920s, Phi Sigma Kappa replaced their old wood-framed facility—located at 31 North Main Street—with this new and far larger brick house, seen here c. 1940. Today, the fraternity house is owned by TAU Corporation.

The Sigma Chi fraternity constructed this Colonial Revival-style house in 1912, but the building was to be short-lived. During the night of September 28, 1931, the fraternity house burned in a fast-moving fire that forced several of the residents to jump for their lives.

Not wishing to risk a repeat of the devastating 1931 fire, Sigma Chi immediately rebuilt their house—this time of brick and fireproof materials. The new building retained much of the general appearance of the original facility.

Phi Delta Theta was the first fraternity to take up residence on the recently opened Webster Avenue. In 1900, they erected this Georgian Revival-style house for themselves (seen here *c.* 1910), and it is still in use today.

The local chapter of the Kappa Sigma fraternity was organized in 1905, and by 1915 they had constructed this stucco Craftsman-style building at 7 Webster Avenue for their use. In 1937 it was replaced by the present brick structure.

The college built a new president's house overlooking Tuck Drive and Webster Avenue in 1926. Designed by Jens Fredrik Larson, the house was paid for by a gift from Edward Tuck. The final expense for the house, grounds, and furnishings was $132,000.

The Sigma Nu fraternity moved from their old house on North Main Street into this new facility at 12 Webster Avenue in 1925. The Georgian Revival-style building was designed by architects Larson & Wells of Hanover.

On January 3, 1929, Delta Tau Delta's new fraternity house at 10 Webster Avenue took fire, and, with the exception of the exterior masonry walls, it was almost a complete ruin. The Georgian Revival-style building was constructed in 1925 from drawings prepared by Blackall, Clapp, and Whittemore Architects of Boston, Massachusetts.

During the 1920s, Zeta Psi erected this new house—similar to others on the Dartmouth Campus—at 8 Webster Avenue. Designed by Larson & Wells Architects, the building was constructed in 1925.

90

Jackson Gould constructed this frame dwelling in 1874 at 36 North Main Street, and for some years it was the home of the Delta Tau Delta fraternity. The building was extensively remodeled in 1963.

This building, now the home of Alpha Theta House Corporation at 33 North Main Street, was for many years the Theta Chi fraternity house. Originally, the house and the structure located immediately north at 35 North Main Street were candy and bakery shops erected by E.K. Smith shortly after the Civil War.

This view *c.* 1905 looking up North Main Street shows the Delta Tau Delta house on the left and Theta Chi on the right. Rope Ferry Road, then an unimproved, rutted, stump-lined country road, stretches off into the distance.

Frank A. Sherman, a mathematics professor at the college, erected this house in 1883 on the outskirts of the village, at today's corner of North Main and Maynard Streets. Originally designed in the rustic, picturesque style favored by mid-century Victorians, by about the 1920s—when the structure was home to the Sigma Phi Epsilon fraternity—the building's out-of-date look was replaced with the chic English Tudor design seen here.

When college President William J. Tucker retired from Dartmouth College in 1909, he erected this sturdy-looking shingled house for himself at 6 Occom Ridge. He resided until his death in 1926.

Dr. Howard N. Kingsford, medical director of the college, built this excellent Shingle-style home in 1905 at 6 Clement Road. By this time, the rolling farmland of the northeastern part of the village was fast disappearing, as stylish new residences continued to be erected.

Webster Avenue was home to Hanover's first modern subdivision, opened up by the college in 1896. Homes on Occom Ridge followed along within a year, pushing their way northward as the college erected contemporary shingled houses for faculty members and their families. This view shows the new development about 1910, looking north from about the intersection of Clement Road.

In 1899, fourteen men purchased a tract of land west of Rope Ferry Road and north of Occom Pond, and hence began the Hanover Country Club. This c. 1910 view looking northeast across Occom Pond shows the golf links along the east side; in the far distance, we can just barely see the new residence of Homer E. Keyes at 37 Rope Ferry Road.

Occom Pond, created in 1900 by clearing and damming a swamp, was largely the creation of two men—Mr. Z.P. Chase and Professor Thomas W.D. Northen. The oval pond, slightly more than 9 acres, contributes the piping melody of a myriad of frogs in the spring and the pleasures of skating in the winter.

At the north end of Occom Pond is the Dartmouth Outing Club Building, a delightful stone structure artfully adapted to the pond and its rolling terrain. Designed by Jens Fredrik Larson and the gift of the Class of 1900, the new building was dedicated in January 1929.

Henry H. Hilton, Class of 1890, was an early benefactor to the Hanover Country Club. Over the years he made additional gifts that in 1916 allowed the clubhouse to be erected. Further gifts from Mr. Hilton purchased additional property, as well as an iron bridge over the brook in the Vale of Tempe in 1921.

This view looks across the golf course from the clubhouse about 1918 toward Pine Park. In 1900, concern that a 45-acre tract of forest land was about to be acquired by the Diamond Match Company and possibly logged prompted a group of citizens to organize the Pine Park Association and raise over $4,000 to purchase the property. And so, it has remained pristine and untouched to this day.

Five

The East Side of the Campus

This c. 1904 view was taken looking southeast across the recently constructed Occom Pond toward the new Mary Hitchcock Memorial Hospital. On the right-hand side of the photograph is Professor Frank A. Sherman's house at the corner of North Main and Maynard Streets.

It is estimated that Hiram Hitchcock spent at least $200,000 of his own money to fund the construction of the new hospital. Completed in 1893, it was a memorial to his late wife, Mary Maynard Hitchcock. The 7-acre site chosen for the new complex was farmland at the time considered outside of the village area. In 1913, a two-story, twenty-seven-bed wing was added, visible to the far left in this *c*. 1915 view.

The new hospital, designed by Rand & Taylor Architects of Boston, Massachusetts, was in every respect a state-of-the-art, fully modern facility. This *c*. 1905 postcard view shows the northeast wing of the complex and the surgical unit containing a high-domed operating theater, which seated 150 persons and was illuminated by a large skylight. In the foreground are fields belonging to the adjacent Dewey farm.

The entire facility was built of fireproof construction with the exception of interior wood trim. This view shows the main stairwell in the center section of the complex. Like all the interior floor structures, the stairways were placed on light masonry tile arches.

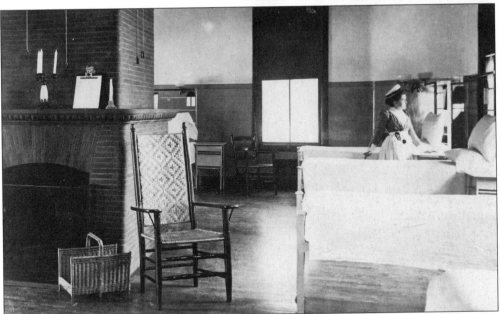

The hospital was one of the first in America designed on the Pavilion Plan; its exterior was modeled on early Italian Renaissance architecture. To either side of the main building were one-story domed wards (one of the two is shown above c. 1905), each accommodating ten patients. The whole capacity of the original complex was thirty-six beds.

The Hitchcock Clinic was established in 1927 by the five doctors that then made up the hospital's entire medical staff. By 1937 the staff had grown, and a separate but attached clinic building was constructed to the west side of the original hospital complex. Designed by Jens Fredrik Larson, the new facility cost $58,699 and was opened in 1938.

This aerial view of the hospital complex looking north in 1943 shows how the facility had grown in fifty years since the completion of the original facility in 1893. By this time, bed capacity was 196; during the previous year, 4,568 patients were treated.

Dick's House, built in 1926 as the college infirmary, was the gift of Mr. and Mrs. Edward K. Hall as a memorial to their son, Richard Drew Hall, who had died of polio during his sophomore year at Dartmouth. The new facility cost $297,655 and was designed by Jens Fredrik Larson.

The Billings-Lee House was built in 1920 as a home for student nurses in the years when the hospital had a nursing school. The $52,847 facility was a gift of the Billings family of Woodstock, Vermont, and was designed and constructed by Edgar H. Hunter.

In 1896, Dr. John M. Gile constructed this fine Colonial Revival-style home on the south side of Maynard Street across from the new hospital. By the time of his death at age sixty-one in 1925, Dr. Gile was widely considered the leading surgeon in the state and was known and loved by many. In later years, his residence became part of the hospital complex—referred to as Fowler House. In 1992 the building was demolished.

Arthur S. Hardy, a professor of civil engineering and mathematics, constructed this rather eclectic home for himself at 43 North College Street in 1876. President Tucker later purchased the property in 1893 and set about constructing additions. In 1909, the college purchased it and used it as the president's home until 1926, when a new facility on Webster Avenue was completed.

Dartmouth Medical College, Hanover, N.H.

The Dartmouth Medical School was established in 1797, the fourth such school established in the country. By 1809, funds were on hand to erect this brick building, completed in 1811. Situated on North College Street where the Burke Chemistry Building is located today, the building was remodeled and received a third floor in 1871. This new floor area was surrounded with continuous high windows which provided natural interior illumination, as can be seen in this c. 1905 view. Sadly, the building was demolished in 1963.

Dr. Nathan Smith was a noted physician of his day and the founder of the Dartmouth Medical School. In 1907, a new laboratory building was erected and named in his memory. The modest, though stylish, structure cost $21,000 and was designed by Edgar H. Hunter, the superintendent of buildings and grounds at the college. In 1990, the building was demolished to make way for the Burke Chemistry Building.

Members of the Dewey family, originally from Springfield, Massachusetts, were some of the earliest settlers in Hanover, and until well into this century, they owned all the land that is today the site of the Dartmouth Medical School. This *c.* 1905 postcard view shows the Dewey farm at the end of North College Street. The house was erected in 1842 by George Dewey; however, the barns were much older. The house was demolished in 1962.

After the destruction of the original Congregational White Church by fire in May 1931, the college provided a site on North College Street for a new structure to be built. Designed by the noted church architect Hobart Upjohn, the construction of the new facility was overseen by Hanover architects Wells, Hudson & Granger. It was dedicated in November 1935.

This c. 1910 postcard view of North College Street was taken looking north from opposite Webster Hall. To the right is the newly completed Wheeler Hall dormitory. The two-story frame dwelling down the street was built by Deacon Benoni Dewey in 1809. In 1916, it became the home of the Sigma Alpha Epsilon fraternity.

SIGMA ALPHA EPSILON HOUSE, DARTMOUTH COLLEGE, HANOVER, N. H.

During the mid- to late 1920s, Sigma Alpha Epsilon removed their old wood-framed building from its 38 North College Street site and constructed this new brick fraternity house.

Abigail Dewey, the widow of William A. Dewey, constructed this frame dwelling on the present site of the east entrance to Baker Library in 1842. By about 1905, when this postcard view was taken, the building had become the Graduate Club. Today the house is located at 24 East Wheelock Street.

In 1816, the college became embroiled in a lawsuit with the State of New Hampshire, questioning whether Dartmouth was a state university or a private institution. During that troubled three-year period, a $1,000 gift from John Wheeler of Orford kept the college going. Therefore, in 1905, this new, ninety-eight-student dormitory was named in his memory. Designed by Charles A. Rich, the new facility cost $83,135.

From 1832, when it was erected by Luke Dewey, until the bitter cold night of January 1, 1918, when it was consumed by a raging fire, this charming stone and brick house stood on North College Street just north of Wheeler Hall. So rapid and hot was the fire that the occupants barely escaped, dressed only in their nightclothes.

When completed in October 1921, the new Steele Chemistry Building was a state-of-the-art facility that, with equipment, cost a total of $475,000. The new building, designed by Larson & Wells Architects, was named for Benjamin H. Steele, Class of 1857. Much of its cost was covered by a bequest of $249,000 from Mr. Steele's brother and college trustee, Sanford Steele.

Charles T. Wilder, who owned large paper mills on the Connecticut River at Wilder, Vermont, left $184,000 in 1897 to the college he never attended. A new physics laboratory building was built in 1898 and named in his honor. The facility cost $84,201 and was designed by Charles A. Rich.

Richardson Hall, erected in 1897, was the first completely new, modern dormitory built on the campus; it housed fifty students in as luxurious accommodations as could be found at any college. The new building was designed by Charles A. Rich at a cost of $49,013 and was named for James B. Richardson, associate justice of the Massachusetts Supreme Court, distinguished alumnus, and college trustee. It is 1914, and the Class of 1864 is in residence for their 50th reunion.

College President Samuel Colcord Bartlett (1877–1892) suggested the construction of Bartlett Tower as a symbol commemorating the fabled "Old Pine" and as a space for college seniors to work off their excess energies. The medieval stone tower, 71 feet high, was begun by the Class of 1885 in that year and finished ten years later by the Class of 1895. This view shows the tower c. 1915.

The "Old Pine," perhaps twenty-five years old when the college was founded in 1770, for many years occupied the summit of the College Park and was an integral part of Dartmouth traditions—especially at graduation time. In 1895, the gnarled old tree, having been wracked by storms and hit by lightening, was finally cut down; however, its stump still survives, as seen in this c. 1905 view.

Views from Bartlett Tower have been popular for almost one hundred years, and this photograph looking southwest out over the campus in 1906 has always been a favorite scene. It has been published in postcard form for many years and illustrates the early twentieth-century evolution of the campus.

Looking west from the tower in the year 1900, the roof of President Tucker's house is in the foreground, the new Mary Hitchcock Memorial Hospital is in the center of the photograph, and up on Occom Ridge, the college is constructing new faculty housing. Within the year, Occom Pond would also be created.

Looking north from the tower up Lyme Road in the late 1890s, one sees the fields of the George Dewey farm in the foreground and the large horse-breeding farm of Harlan P. Flint in the center of this view. Today, most of Mr. Flint's farm is part of the Hanover Country Club.

Looking east from the tower in the late 1890s, one can see East Wheelock Street working its way up Balch Hill and out to Etna Village. The farm to the left center of this view was once part of the stone house that still survives today at 1 Rip Road, originally constructed by Professor Alpheus Crosby about 1845.

Looking from the tower southwest down onto the intersection of East Wheelock and Park Streets in the late 1890s, one can plainly see the large farm of John M. Fuller, as well as several stylish new residences constructed about ten years prior on North Park Street. Mr. Fuller's farm was, until 1893, part of the New Hampshire College of Agriculture and Mechanical Arts—later known as UNH.

The Shattuck Observatory, seen here c. 1915, was constructed in 1852 from plans prepared by architect Ammi B. Young. Made possible by monetary gifts from Dr. George C. Shattuck, Class of 1803 and a noted Boston physician, the final cost of the building was slightly in excess of $4,800. Much of the expense can be attributed to the care required to fabricate the revolving dome.

Once the college had the benefit of an integrated and abundant water supply system (which was in operation by 1893), planning began for the construction of modern, sanitary dormitory facilities. Richardson Hall was the first such building to be constructed of masonry, and the Fayerweather complex was the second. Together these three buildings providing housing for 285 students at a cost of $110,276.

The central Fayerweather dormitory was the first building constructed in the complex. It was made possible by gifts from the estate of Daniel B. Fayerweather that would eventually total $223,000. Erected in 1900, the new building cost $44,060, was designed by Charles A. Rich, and provided space for eighty-five students.

113

North Fayerweather, constructed with its twin South Fayerweather in 1907, was likewise designed by Charles A. Rich. The new building, which cost $30,530 and housed one hundred students, barely escaped destruction by fire less than a year later.

South Fayerweather, shown here playing host to the Class of 1879 at their 35th reunion, was, like the rest of the complex, thought at the time to embody the height of architectural style in its Colonial Revival beauty. Compare this building to the already dated Victorian-styled Culver Hall beside it to the right.

During the bitter cold night of February 26, 1910, the South Fayerweather dormitory caught fire, and the fast-moving blaze barely allowed the students time to escape. Luckily, there were no serious injuries, although some of the residents had to jump for their lives from windows into deep snow.

South Fayerweather's spectacular blaze prompted the publication of several postcards showing the destruction. In the aftermath, the college made the decision that all future dormitories would be designed of fire-resistant materials with a high regard for fire safety.

Bartlett Hall was constructed in 1890 as a facility for the Young Men's Christian Association. Designed in the Romanesque Revival style by architect Lambert Packard, of St. Johnsbury, Vermont, the building cost about $17,000 and was named for retiring college President Samuel Colcord Bartlett.

Culver Hall was erected in 1870 by the State of New Hampshire as part of their College of Agriculture and the Mechanical Arts, which was located in Hanover from 1867 until 1893, when the college moved to Durham and became UNH. This classroom building was designed by Edward Dow of Concord and was purchased in 1893 by Dartmouth and used by the college until it was torn down in 1929. By then it was just a frumpy old Victorian building.

The Bema (the Greek word for "sanctuary") was created under the direction of President Bartlett in 1882. Built as an outdoor amphitheater, it was the site of all college commencements from the time of its completion until 1953, when the June exercises were shifted to the front lawn of Baker Library.

RIPLEY, WOODWARD AND SMITH HALLS, DARTMOUTH COLLEGE, HANOVER, N. H.

Ripley, Woodward, and Smith Halls were some of the last buildings to be completed during the building boom that took place on the campus in the 1920s under the direction of President Hopkins. First occupied in 1930, this complex of three buildings housed 169 students and was designed by Jens Fredrik Larson. All three facilities together cost $260,000 and were named for three of the first professors at the college in the 1770s.

In 1903, the Sphinx Society had this truly unique structure erected on a bluff overlooking East Wheelock Street. Designed in the Egyptian Revival style, this small battered-wall building is constructed almost entirely of poured concrete. During the 1920s, an addition was made to the rear of the building.

Alumni Gymnasium, Dartmouth College, Hanover, N. H.

When Alumni Gymnasium opened, it was considered the most complete facility of its kind in the eastern states. Constructed in 1909 from plans prepared by Charles A. Rich, the new $190,000 building was largely financed by Dartmouth Alumni subscription.

118

Alpha Delta Phi House, Dartmouth College.
HANOVER, N. H.

The first building erected in the village specifically for a fraternity house was this structure constructed by Alpha Delta Phi in 1872. The unique Italianate brick building cost $4,000 and was located at 9 East Wheelock Street until it was demolished in 1921 to make room for the much larger present house.

ALPHA DELTA PHI HOUSE, DARTMOUTH COLLEGE, HANOVER, N. H.

In 1922, after the removal of their old building, the Alpha Delta Phi fraternity constructed this much larger house at the same location. Designed in the popular Georgian Revival style, the facility was of fireproof construction, like so many other fraternity houses erected on campus during the decade of the 1920s.

This Second Empire-style building actually began life at the corner of Main and Wheelock Streets, now occupied by College Hall. Erected by Richard Lang in 1795 as a late Georgian-style home of fine proportions, it was moved to this location at 11 East Wheelock Street in 1875. Within a year, it was renovated to become the home we see here. In 1911, the Chi Phi fraternity bought the property, utilizing the house until moving it away in 1927 to allow the construction of a larger facility.

CHI PHI HOUSE, DARTMOUTH COLLEGE, HANOVER, N. H.

After the removal of their old building to 23 South Park Street in August 1927, Chi Phi began construction on this new and far larger house. The facility was completed in June 1928, and it cost a total of $40,000, all of which was acquired through a diligent and aggressive fund-raising effort.

New Hampshire Hall was the last and the largest dormitory constructed during the Tucker Administration (1893–1909). Designed by Charles A. Rich, the new facility cost $80,000 and housed 107 students. Named for all New Hampshire alumni, it was hoped that they would contribute to the building's cost.

President Tucker realized that only with a central heating plant could the college expand as he was planning. Built in 1898 at a cost of $77,000, this building was designed by Charles A. Rich and was the first such collegiate facility in the northeast. Eventually, eight coal-fired steam boilers provided heat to thirty-nine college buildings through 7,900 feet of steam lines.

This Italianate-style structure was erected in 1874 as a dormitory and dining hall for the state's agricultural school and named Conant Hall. In 1892, Dartmouth acquired the building, renaming it Hallgarten Hall after a college benefactor. By 1925, after the completion of Topliff Hall, the front portion of the never-popular building was torn down.

In 1920, the fashionable Topliff Hall was built in front of the unfashionable Victorian Hallgarten Hall. Designed by Jens Fredrik Larson, the new facility cost $355,000 and was the largest dormitory on campus, sleeping 235 students. The building was named for Elijah M. Topliff of Manchester, New Hampshire, Class of 1852, who in 1917 had bequeathed the college $240,000.

When the State of New Hampshire decided to move its school to Durham in 1893, Dartmouth purchased the 25 acres in Hanover that now contain athletic fields. That year, 10 acres were developed into a combination baseball/football field—paid for by alumni subscription. This view looks north toward East Wheelock Street *c.* 1905.

In addition to grading the field, Dartmouth erected a cinder oval running track and a wooden grandstand. Here we see the Dartmouth baseball team beating arch rival Harvard 6 to 4 in May 1908.

The Davis Varsity Field House was the gift of Howard Clark Davis, Class of 1906, of Boston, Massachusetts. Built in 1926, the $138,000 facility was designed by Jens Fredrik Larson in the favored Georgian Revival style. Mr. Davis also gave $60,000 for a hockey rink, which has since been demolished.

By the early 1920s, the college's athletic fields were in deplorable condition. As a result, the alumni raised $225,000 to be put toward a memorial stadium honoring the 112 Dartmouth men who lost their lives in World War I. The new stadium was designed by Jens Fredrik Larson, was built in 1922, and with related work to the field, cost $257,000.

This curious brick building on South Park Street was originally constructed in 1889 by the State of New Hampshire as an experimental station for the agricultural school. By 1894, after the state school had left Hanover, the Thayer School of Engineering paid $3,714 for the building that had five years earlier cost the state $7,000.

Development along South Park Street was beginning to fill out when this photograph was taken from the Velvet Rocks during the summer of 1905. Professor Frank E. Austin's residence at 11 South Park Street can be seen under construction—it was the first house erected in the village with a poured concrete foundation.

This writer has not been able to determine what the "Society Circus" was; however, regardless of the event, it merited a postcard *c.* 1910. The parade is heading north up Crosby Street; in the background is the old wooden stadium at the Alumni Oval.

Exactly what this scene represents, this author is not quite sure. However, the caption on the postcard reads: "Dartmouth Prom May 1907." The photograph was taken close to South Park Street, about where the Leverone Field House is today.

Park Street is a very old road that was laid out early in the village's development, although houses were not built along the street until 1884. This postcard view, taken about 1910 looking north from the Wheelock Street intersection, shows several houses built in 1903 and 1906. For years, until it was first paved, Park Street was one of the worst mud holes in the village each spring.

This postcard view c. 1920 looks north up Lyme Road from just beyond the Park Street intersection. Actually, this state highway is representative of the best roads in the region during the early years of this century.

And so we leave this very special place, with one last glimpse at an aerial postcard view taken in 1922 looking north at the village below. In the foreground are the fields of the Currier farm, spreading from South Main Street at the left to Lebanon Street at the right. In the center of the photograph is the College Green.